Lost Railways of
Co. Down and Co. Armagh

by
Stephen Johnson

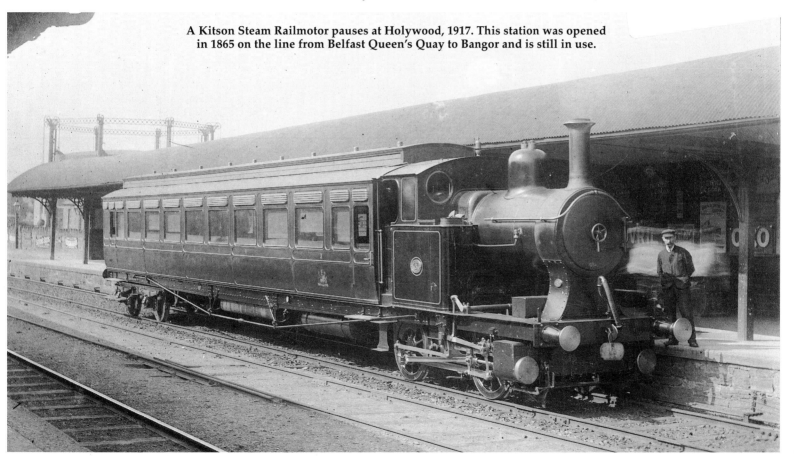

A Kitson Steam Railmotor pauses at Holywood, 1917. This station was opened in 1865 on the line from Belfast Queen's Quay to Bangor and is still in use.

PICTURE ACKNOWLEDGEMENTS
The publishers wish to thank the following for contributing pictures to this book: John Alsop for pages 26, 43, 44 and 45; R.M. Casserley for the front cover and pages 7, 8, 10, 18, 19, 29–35, 38, and 42 (these photographs were taken by H.C. Casserley); Ian McCullough for pages 1, 14, 15, 22, 39, 46, and the back cover; Des Quail for the inside front cover, pages 2, 4–6, 9, 11–13, 16, 17, 20, 21, 24, 25, 27, 36, 37, 40, 41, 47, and the inside back cover; and W.A.C. Smith for pages 3 and 48. The pictures on pages 23 and 28 are from the publisher's own collection. Thanks also to Neville Stead for his help and advice.

Opened in 1863, this station replaced two earlier stations. First served by the Ulster Railway in 1842, Portadown still retains a train service on the busy Dublin–Belfast main line, albeit at a different station which opened in 1970.

INTRODUCTION

Co. Down and Co. Armagh, once busy with railway traffic, have but two lines left between them: the interstate railway between Dublin and Belfast, and the busy commuter line from Belfast to Bangor. Translink, part of the Northern Ireland Transport Holdings Group, now operate the services that are left, but over half a century ago the two counties boasted numerous lines serving all parts of the country, operated by the Great Northern Railway of Ireland (GNR(I)) and the Belfast & Co. Down Railway (BCDR).

The railways in Co. Armagh developed somewhat differently from those of Co. Down as they were built by a number of smaller companies and were gradually absorbed over a period into the GNR(I). In contrast, Co. Down's were almost all built by the BCDR.

The railways of the two counties had their fair share of oddities and claims to fame. Co. Armagh could boast the Bessbrook & Newry Tramway, the first all-year-round service by electric railway, as well as the longest tunnel in Ireland, and also endured the infamy of the Markethill Disaster which did so much to change railway operating practice. Co. Down, on the other hand, had busy commuter lines, the renowned non-stop 'Golfer's Express' to the popular resort of Newcastle, and the unusual stations and triangular junction at Downpatrick.

The demise of the railways in these counties started in 1950 with the wholesale closure of the BCDR by the Ulster Transport Authority (UTA), a concern which favoured road transport. Meanwhile, post-war financial difficulties threatened the GNR(I), forcing the island's two governments to bail out the ailing company in 1953. This bought just a few years for the Great Northern Railway Board, as the GNR(I) became, before it too was forced to start closing lines. In 1958 the company was disbanded and the assets split between the two state operators. The lines in Éire went to Córas Iompair Éireann (CIE) and those in Northern Ireland went to the UTA.

This book begins with Co. Down, looking at the closed routes of the former BCDR. The main route from Belfast Queen's Quay to Comber, Downpatrick, Newcastle and the branch to Ballynahinch are examined first, followed by the route from Comber to Donaghadee, and the short branch to Ardglass and its harbour. Sections on the GNR(I)'s two lines which ran into Co. Down follow: the

short branch from Scarva on the Dublin to Belfast line to the town of Banbridge, and the route from Knockmore Junction via Banbridge to Newcastle, where the GNR(I) met the BCDR at Castlewellan.

Moving into Co. Armagh, the unique little Bessbrook & Newry Tramway is examined first before turning to the lines operated by the GNR(I). First is the line from Goraghwood, on the Dublin to Belfast line, to the important town and port of Newry and the resorts of Warrenpoint and Rostrevor. Returning to Goraghwood, the narrative travels in the opposite direction over the hills to Armagh and looks at one of the shortest-lived lines in Ireland, the route to Castleblaney. Portadown was once an important junction with two routes to Londonderry, one via Armagh and the other via Pomeroy; these are covered, before the final sections look at some of the closed stations which stood on the existing Dublin to Belfast line and the route from Belfast to Bangor.

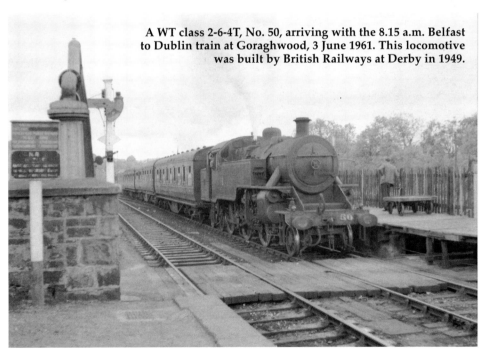

A WT class 2-6-4T, No. 50, arriving with the 8.15 a.m. Belfast to Dublin train at Goraghwood, 3 June 1961. This locomotive was built by British Railways at Derby in 1949.

Co. Down

Belfast Queen's Quay – Ballynahinch & Newcastle

Passenger service withdrawn 24 April 1950 (Belfast to Comber) /
16 January 1950 (Comber to Ballynahinch & Newcastle)
Distance 38 miles
Company Belfast & Co. Down Railway

Stations closed	*Date*
Belfast Queen's Quay *	12 April 1976
Fraser Street Halt **	24 April 1950
Bloomfield	24 April 1950
Neill's Hill	24 April 1950
Knock ***	24 April 1950
Dundonald	24 April 1950
Henryville Halt ****	1936
Comber	24 April 1950
Ballygowan	16 January 1950
Shephard's Bridge Halt	16 January 1950

Stations closed	*Date*
Saintfield	16 January 1950
Ballynahinch branch	
Ballynahinch Junction	16 January 1950
Creevyargon Halt	16 January 1950
Ballynahinch	16 January 1950
Crossgar	16 January 1950
King's Bridge Halt	1942
Downpatrick *****	16 January 1950
Downpatrick Loop Platform *****	16 January 1950
Tullymurray	16 January 1950
Ballykinlar Halt †	16 January 1950
Dundrum	16 January 1950
Newcastle ††	16 January 1950

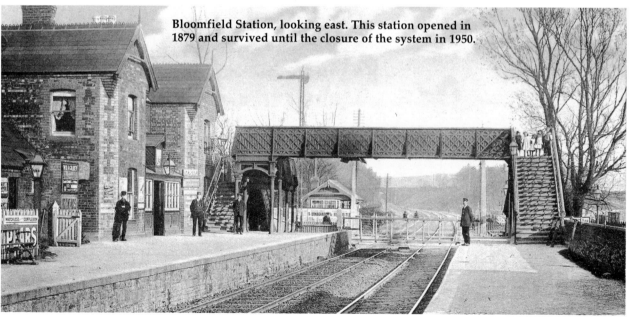

Bloomfield Station, looking east. This station opened in 1879 and survived until the closure of the system in 1950.

* Although Comber services ceased on 24 April 1950, this station remained open until 1976 to serve the Bangor line until replaced by Belfast Central Station.

** Fraser Street had an Up platform only.

*** Known as Knock & Belmont, 1865/6–1888/9.

**** Henryville Halt was a temporary station used during the TT Car races between 1928 and 1936.

***** These stations were reopened in 1990 by the Downpatrick and Ardglass Railway, a preserved steam railway.

† Ballykinlar Halt served an army camp and was not advertised to the public.

†† Newcastle was closed to UTA trains in 1950 but remained open to GNR(I) trains until 1955.

Neill's Hill Station, looking east. Opened in 1890, this was one of the four intermediate stations built after the opening of the line to Comber in 1850.

The BCDR served the central and eastern parts of Co. Down and managed to remain an independent concern from its inception in 1846 until October 1948, when it became part of the UTA. These new owners managed to close all but just over twelve miles of track by April 1950. The BCDR started with a short stretch of track from Belfast to Holywood which opened in August 1848. In 1846 the company had obtained powers to push south to Comber, Newtonards and Newcastle and the line to Comber opened on 6 May 1850 with an intermediate station at Dundonald (Knock opened later that year). By then the original powers to complete the line to Newcastle had lapsed and fresh powers were required, so it was not until 1855 that the project got going again.

Knock Station, looking east. This station opened in late 1850.

The extension to Ballynahinch from a junction at Comber opened on 10 September 1858, with stations at Ballygowan and Saintfield. Then the line was again extended southwards to Downpatrick, although this extension commenced a little further up the line from Ballynahinch. The result was that when the Downpatrick line opened on 23 March 1859, Ballynahinch found itself at the end of a three and a half mile branch. The junction was provided with a station called Ballynahinch Junction and one station at Crossgar opened with the extension. In 1930 a new halt was provided on the branch at Creevyargon.

Ballynahinch Junction Station, 17 April 1948. The branch train is standing at the platform for the service to Ballynahinch.

On 25 March 1869 the line from Downpatrick to Newcastle opened with one intermediate station at Dundrum. The route of the line left Downpatrick as a terminus station so that reversal was necessary for any through Belfast–Newcastle services. (This line was built by a separate company, the Downpatrick, Dundrum & Newcastle Railway, although the line was worked by the BCDR and ended up being absorbed by that company in 1881.) The Downpatrick Loop, built to avoid the reversal of through trains, opened on 24 September 1892. An exchange platform was provided at the south of the loop and it soon became common practise for passengers to change here from the main line train to a branch train to reach Downpatrick town.

With the arrival of the railway the fortunes of Newcastle were improved. The BCDR were keen to promote the town's status as a resort and provided a large 120 room hotel, the Slieve Donard, in 1898 (it was sold by the UTA in 1966). More stations were also added to the route – Bloomfield in 1879, Neill's Hill in 1890, and Tullymurray in 1871 (this last one was replaced by a new station in 1896) – and one of the best known trains to run on the BCDR was the unofficially titled Golfer's Express. Departing from Belfast at noon on Saturdays, this non-stop train took 50 minutes to reach Newcastle, slipping a coach at Comber for Donaghadee. Further special sports-related services were ran between 1928 and 1936 when the Royal Automobile Club ran their Tourist Trophy Race around north Co. Down. The BCDR provided a temporary halt at Henryville for the week and even built a grandstand at Comber, but the races were discontinued when nine spectators were killed in a crash.

Dundrum Station, *c*.1909. This opened in 1869 on the Downpatrick, Dundrum & Newcastle Railway which was absorbed into the BCDR in 1881.

Meanwhile, the line continued operating its services without major incident, adding more halts at Fraser Street in 1928, King's Bridge in 1929, Shepherd's Bridge in 1930 (Ballykinlar Halt opened in 1914 to serve a local army camp, although it was not advertised to the public). However, the junction at Ballymacarrett, just outside Queen's Quay Station, saw one of Ireland's worst railway accidents in 1945 when a rear end collision in fog caused 23 deaths.

Newcastle Station served as a terminus for both the BCDR and the GNR(I). The station clock tower is visible behind the station with the Mountains of Mourne looming beyond.

When the UTA acquired the railway, at a price of just £485,990, they didn't waste much time in closing it. For forty years the line remained unused, but on 7 May 1990 the section between Downpatrick, the Loop Platform and South Junction was reopened by the Downpatrick & Ardglass Railway. This was formed by enthusiasts with the aim of restoring the line around the Downpatrick area and by 1995 the group, now called the Downpatrick Steam Railway, had extended southwards to a new halt called Magnus' Grave just short of Ardglass Junction.

Comber – Donaghadee

Passenger service withdrawn	24 April 1950
Distance	14.5 miles
Company	Belfast & Co. Down Railway

Stations closed	*Date*
Comber	24 April 1950
Glass Moss Road *	1936
Newtonards (Church Street)	3 June 1861
Newtonards	24 April 1950

Stations closed	*Date*
Conlig	1873
Ballygrainey **	24 April 1950
Ballyfotherly	*c.*1876
Millisle Road Halt	24 April 1950
Donaghadee	24 April 1950

* A temporary station serving the TT races between 1928 and 1936.
** Formerly called Groomsport & Bangor, then Groomsport Road.

Comber Station, looking south. Here the line splits with a route going to Newcastle and another to Donaghadee.

The approach to the second station built at Newtonards on the extension to Donaghadee. Built of local sandstone from the Scrabo Quarries, it opened on 3 June 1861.

The line to Donaghadee was part of the original construction from Belfast to Newtonards. From Comber, the line turned around sharply and faced north-east on its way to Newtonards. A terminus station was built off Newtonards' Church Street to accommodate the service and the line opened on 6 May 1850. In the meantime, the Admiralty recommended that the coastal town of Donaghadee be provided with a harbour and this was financed by the Treasury so that short sea crossings to Portpatrick in Scotland could be made.

Newtonards Station, looking towards Belfast. Although modernised in 1896, the station remained awkward to work.

The BCDR commenced extending their railway from Newtonards to Donaghadee with the help of a large loan. A new station was provided at Newtonards on the extension and the line was opened on 3 June 1861. Stations were provided at Conlig and Ballygrainey. The harbour was opened in 1863, but it took until March 1870 before the BCDR had opened their short half mile harbour spur to meet it. Storms in 1865 left Portpatrick unsuitable as a port and the government switched their support to the Stranraer to Larne route. A steamship company was set up to operate between Portpatrick and Donaghadee, but soon gave up due to the difficulties at Portpatrick. All this left the BCDR with a large loan to pay off and little of the promised income. However, the Government gave the BCDR a loan at a lower rate of interest as recompense.

Newtonards Station, looking west. A Belfast-bound train looks as if it was getting plenty of custom.

The harbour line was out of use by the 1930s but wasn't officially closed until the closure of the line as a whole. A station at Ballyfotherly was opened around 1863 but closed again about 1876. In 1928 the RAC TT race came to Co. Down. The race course crossed the railway at four locations: three bridges and one level crossing. The crossing was at Glass Moss Road, a mile and a half from Comber.

Donaghadee Station, the terminus of the line. Built in 1904, the Beyer Peacock 4-4-2T, No. 12, stands at the platform with a Belfast-bound train.

The BCDR were quite co-operative with the race organisers and provided a temporary station for the duration of the races, even to the extent of interrupting the Donaghadee service. A platform was erected each side of the crossing with a footbridge across the line. During racing, a shuttle service was operated on either side, through passengers having to use the footbridge for the connection. The station closed in 1936 after the races had been discontinued. Millisle Road Halt was also opened in 1928 and survived until the closure of the line which came on 24 April 1950 when the entire route from Belfast was closed by the UTA.

Ardglass Junction – Ardglass

			Stations closed	Date
Passenger service withdrawn	16 January 1950		Bright Halt	16 January 1950
Distance	8.25 miles		Killough	16 January 1950
Company	Belfast & Co. Down Railway		Coney Island Halt	*c.*1942
			Ardglass	16 January 1950
Stations closed	*Date*			
Race Course Platform (Downpatrick) *	16 January 1950		* This was open on race days only.	
Ballynoe	16 January 1950			

Killough Station opened on 8 July 1892. It featured a sharp ten chain curve through the platform.

In the 1880s the government was keen to promote trade and commerce in Ireland and appointed a royal commission, chaired by Sir James Allport, general manager of the Midland Railway, to look into promoting the building of railway lines to, amongst other places, small fishing villages like Ardglass. As a result of this commission's recommendations, the BCDR were contracted to build a railway to Ardglass. In 1890 the Downpatrick, Killough & Ardglass Light Railway was set up for the purpose with a free grant of £29,980 and a 3% baronial guarantee of £17,000. Economically built, the line opened for goods traffic on 27 May 1892, with passenger traffic following on 8 July the same year. The line left the main BCDR route just south of Downpatrick at a point called Ardglass Junction. Two intermediate stations at Ballynoe and Killough opened with the line. The racecourse at Downpatrick is adjacent to this line and a special platform, first used on the 8 March 1893, was provided for race traffic. Bright Halt was opened in 1925 with another halt, Coney Island Halt, opening in 1934. However, this one didn't last long as the 1942–43 working timetable states that 'train are not to call'. The half mile harbour tramway, which ran from the end of the station and through the streets of Ardglass to the harbour, fell out of use in the 1920s and was closed by 1932. When the BCDR became part of the UTA the branch suffered the same fate as the rest of the system, closing entirely on 16 January 1950.

Scarva – Banbridge

Passenger service withdrawn	2 May 1955		*Stations closed*	*Date*
Distance	6.75 miles		Laurencetown	2 May 1955
Company	Great Northern Railway of Ireland		Chapel Row Crossing *	1945
			Hazelbank Crossing *	2 May 1955
Stations closed	*Date*		Lenaderg	2 May 1955
Martin's Bridge *	2 May 1955		Smyth's Siding	1929
Kernon Crossing *	2 May 1955		Millmount Crossing *	2 May 1955
Drumhork Crossing *	2 May 1955		Banbridge	30 April 1956
Uprichards Crossing *	1946		* Railcar stopping place.	

Hazelbank Crossing, near Laurencetown. The crossing can just be seen at the end of the bridge. The line was closed in 1933, but reopened in late 1934. When reopened, it was served by a railcar and a number of additional stops were added at level crossings such as this.

The 9.30 a.m. service from Newcastle to Belfast at Banbridge, 18 April 1953. Built at Dundalk in 1911, No. 25 started off life as a PP class locomotive. It was rebuilt in 1927 with a superheater and became a PPs class.

Although on the main highway between Dublin and Belfast, the railway missed the linen and manufacturing town of Banbridge. As a result, the Banbridge, Newry, Dublin & Belfast Junction Railway was formed in 1853 to remedy the situation. Despite the impressively long title, the line was only 6½ miles long, meeting the Dublin & Belfast Junction Railway at Scarva Station (which is still open on the main Dublin–Belfast line). The line opened on the 23 March 1859, having changed its title to the shorter Banbridge Junction Railway, and was worked by the D&BJR. The company had one station at Laurencetown, four miles from Scarva. In the meantime, a more direct route to Belfast was built in the form of the Banbridge, Lisburn & Belfast Railway and the Banbridge Junction Railway was extended to meet this line at a new station in Banbridge which opened in October 1863. The GNR(I) acquired the line in 1877 and in 1904 they added additional stations at Lenaderg and Smyth's Siding. The latter only lasted a few years, closing around 1929. A strike by railway workers in 1933 over pay saw the end of the passenger service on the line, although it was restored in 1934 when the GNR(I) used a railbus to work the line. Along with the revamped service came five new railbus stops at Drumhork, Uprichards, Chapel Row, Hazelbank and Millmount Level Crossings. Martin's Bridge was added in 1937, with Kernan Crossing following in 1953. Chapel Row Crossing was used until 1940, but remained available until 1945 for American troops stationed nearby. The railbus ceased to call at Uprichards Crossing in 1946. The UTA operated a competing bus service after the war and the GNR(I) eventually had to close the line.

Knockmore Junction – Newcastle

Passenger service withdrawn	30 April 1956 (Knockmore Junction to Banbridge)
	2 May 1955 (Banbridge to Newcastle)
Distance	37.25 miles
Company	Great Northern Railway of Ireland / Belfast & Co. Down Railway

Stations closed	*Date*
Canal Bridge *	*c.*1877
Newport Halt	30 April 1956
Hillsborough	30 April 1956
Ballygowan Halt	30 April 1956
Magherabeg	30 April 1956
Dromore	30 April 1956

Stations closed	*Date*
Ashfield	30 April 1956
Mullafernaghan	30 April 1956
Banbridge	30 April 1956
Corbet	2 May 1955
Poland's Bridge	2 May 1955
Katesbridge	2 May 1955
Ballyroney	2 May 1955
Drumadonald	2 May 1955
Ballyward	2 May 1955
Leitrim	2 May 1955
Savage's Bridge	2 May 1955
Castlewellan	2 May 1955
Newcastle	2 May 1955

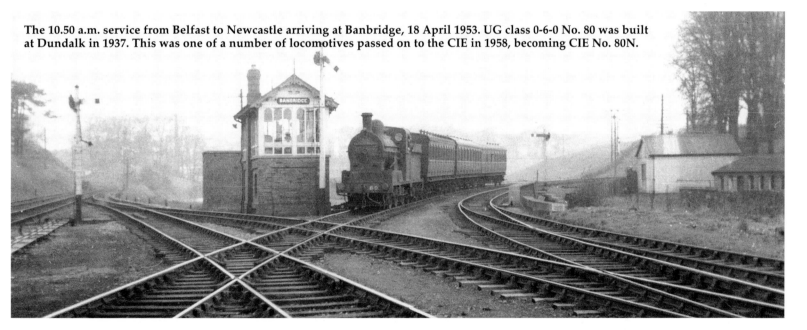

The 10.50 a.m. service from Belfast to Newcastle arriving at Banbridge, 18 April 1953. UG class 0-6-0 No. 80 was built at Dundalk in 1937. This was one of a number of locomotives passed on to the CIE in 1958, becoming CIE No. 80N.

* This was a stopping point for Maze racegoers, certainly during the Belfast, Lisburn & Banbridge Railway period.

Katesbridge Station, _c._1904. This station opened on 14 December 1880 as part of the GNR(I)'s extension at Ballyroney. The minimal facilities can clearly be seen – one platform, a passing loop and a good shed.

Katesbridge

Although the town of Banbridge had managed to get a railway connection to Belfast through the Banbridge Junction Railway via Scarva, it was thought a more direct route would be advantageous. To this end, the Belfast, Lisburn & Banbridge Railway was formed in 1858 to connect Banbridge with the Ulster Railway near Lisburn. Work was slow and the line did not open until 13 July 1863. The line left the Ulster Railway at Knockmore Junction, 1½ miles west of Lisburn. Stations were provided at Hillsborough, Dromore and Mullafernaghan. Near Hillsborough, a 1:57 bank gave the GNR(I) the steepest grade on their system.

Katesbridge eight years later, by which time it had acquired another platform and a signal box.

Shortly after opening, a junction was made with the Banbridge Junction Railway and their trains used the new BL&BR station. While the line was being built, an extension was already being considered by the Banbridge Extension Railway to Castlewellan. In the event, the BER were only allowed to build as far as Ballyroney and even though work was started the company went bankrupt in 1865, having built just eight miles of railway. In 1877, the BL&BR and BJR became part of the GNR(I) and the BER project was given a new lease of life. Completed by the GNR(I), the line opened on the 14 December 1880. One station at Katesbridge was provided, with another at Corbet opening in 1882.

The approach to Ballyroney Station.

It took another twenty years for the line to reach Newcastle, which had expanded greatly as a result of the rival BCDR's efforts. However, it was not to be quite that simple for the GNR(I) to get there. The BCDR sought to close the gap themselves and get running powers over the GNR(I) to Scarva, but a compromise was reached whereby both companies would share the building of the line, meeting at Castlewellan. The GNR(I) got running powers into Newcastle as it wanted and the BCDR got running powers to Ballyroney. Although this was a fair exchange for mileage, the BCDR considered it useless for traffic as Ballyroney consisted of just over half a dozen houses. The line opened on the 24 March 1906 with stations at Ballyward and Leitrim. In 1929, the GNR(I) added more stations along the route at Ballygowan and Maherabeg, while 1930 saw the opening of Ashfield Station with Poland's Bridge and Savage's Bridge opening in 1932. Drumadonald was opened in 1933 and the last station, at Newport, opened in 1942.

Ballyroney was the terminus of the line for 26 years until the extension to Newcastle was opened in 1906.

The lifting of wartime restrictions on fuel allowed UTA bus services to compete with the route to Newcastle and in May 1955 the Banbridge to Newcastle section was closed. The remainder did not last long after this. All that was left was a quarter mile spur from Knockmore Junction to Newforge Siding which served the Burnhouse Rendering Factory, but this too closed with the cessation of freight on the UTA system in 1965.

A GNR(I) BT class 4-4-0T, No. 6, arriving at Ballyroney, *c*.1908. Built in 1869, this locomotive was rebuilt in 1910 and finally withdrawn ten years later.

Although Castlewellan was a through station, the GNR(I) owned the line to the north while the BCDR owned the line south to Newcastle. The GNR(I) used its running powers over the BCDR metals to Newcastle.

GNR(I) PP class No. 71 'Bundoran' standing at Newcastle Station. Although this station was owned by the BCDR, the GNR(I) had running powers over BCDR metals from Castlewellan to Newcastle and ran an alternative service to Belfast via Banbridge.

Co. Armagh

Bessbrook – Newry

Passenger service withdrawn	12 January 1948
Distance	3 miles
Company	Bessbrook & Newry Tramway

Stations closed	*Date*
Bessbrook	12 January 1948
Maytown *	12 January 1948

Stations closed	*Date*
Millvale	12 January 1948
Craigmore	12 January 1948
Newry	12 January 1948

* Formerly Maytown & Mullaghglass and later Mullaghglass & Derramore. Renamed Maytown in 1901.

The tramway terminus at Bessbrook. The car shed can be seen behind the platform. The Bessbrook & Newry Tramway provided the first all-year-round electric service in the British Isles.

The platform of Bessbrook terminus can be seen to the right of the shed. The five rails can clearly be seen. The centre rail was the conductor rail while the outer rails guided the flangeless wagons. One of the Hurst Nelson-built cars stands on the left.

Opened on 1 October 1885, this 3 feet gauge electric tramway ran 3 miles from the mill town of Bessbrook to a point adjacent to Edward Street Station in Newry. Electrified at 245V D.C. by a centre rail, the tramcars also had bow collectors to allow them to traverse the 50 yards long Millvale Crossing using an overhead wire. The trackwork was particularly unusual as there were no less than five parallel rails! The reason for this was that the tramway employed special flangeless-wheeled wagons. These ran on the running rails and were guided by the slightly higher outer rails. The centre rail was the electricity conductor rail. These flangeless wagons could also be used on roads.

Tramcar No. 1 standing at the Bessbrook Terminus in June 1932. This was built by Hurst Nelson in 1921 and was actually the second car to carry the number 1. It replaced an original 1885 Ashbury-built car. The Bow Collector can clearly be seen. This was used to traverse the fifty yard Millvale Crossing by collecting power from an overhead trolley system.

The tramway had the distinction of being the first all-year-round electric service in the British Isles. Running down from Bessbrook, the trams called at Maytown and then Millvale where the bow collector would be raised for traversing the Crossing. Once over, the third rail was again used and the trams would descend towards the next stop at Craigmore, passing under the GNR(I)'s impressive 140 feet high Craigmore Viaduct on the way. After a descent of 190 feet, the trams would arrive at Newry. On the 12 January 1948, the line finally closed after suffering competition from the bus service operated by the Northern Ireland Road Transport Board.

GNR(I)'s Dundalk-built PGs No. 11 'Dromore' standing at Newry Shed, 18 April 1953. Built in 1903, this Clifford designed 0-6-0 tender engine was rebuilt by Glover in 1924. The rebuilding included the addition of a superheater. No. 11 survived into UTA days before being withdrawn in 1960.

Goraghwood – Warrenpoint

Passenger service withdrawn	4 January 1965	*Stations closed*	*Date*
Distance	10.25 miles	Newry Dublin Bridge	4 January 1965
Company	Great Northern Railway of Ireland	Newry Kilmorey Street	2 September 1861
		Green Island	1850
Stations closed	*Date*	Narrow Water Halt	1959
Goraghwood	4 January 1965	Warrenpoint	4 January 1965
Newry Edward Street	4 January 1965		

The signalbox at Goraghwood, 18 April 1953. Goraghwood was where the Newry–Armagh line crossed over the Dublin–Belfast line. Arriving with a train from Warrenpoint is the GNR(I) locomotive No. 127, 'Erebus', a North British-built 4-4-0 of 1907.

A GNR(I) Ps class 4-4-0, No. 89, standing at the platform of Newry Edward Street Station, 4 June 1932. The locomotive was built in 1904 and had a superheater added in 1923. It was withdrawn in 1956.

Although just over ten miles long, this was an amalgam of lines built by three different railway companies. The first section of the route, built by the Newry, Warrenpoint & Rostrevor Railway, opened on 28 May 1849. The line ran from a station at Kilmorey Street in Newry and, despite the company's title, only got as far as Warrenpoint, some six miles away along a fairly even grade on the north shore of Carlingford Lough. The NW&RR never did build the line to Rostrevor, leaving the connection to a narrow gauge tramway.

Newry Edward Street Station, looking south towards Warrenpoint with Edward Street level crossing visible, 18 April, 1953. The Bessbrook & Newry Tramway terminus was just outside the station.

The next part of the story is the Newry & Enniskillen Railway's desire to build a line connecting the places in its title. Work started in Newry on 17 August 1846, but progress was slow and the railway wasn't ready to open until 7 January 1854. Even then, due to a shortage of rolling stock, it took until 1 March to get trains running. The line ran from Edward Street Station in Newry up a 3½ mile climb to meet the Dublin & Belfast Junction Railway at Goraghwood. An extension to the line was built at the Newry end to the Albert Street Basin for goods traffic and was in use by 1854.

GNR(I) Ps class No. 89 waiting at Warrenpoint Station
with the 4.10 p.m. departure to Armagh, 4 June 1962.

The third part of the story lies with the Town of Newry Connecting Railway. Authorised in 1857, this line used 29 chains of the N&ER Albert Street Basin line to King Street. Here a junction was made and a further 57 chains laid, crossing both the canal and river, to a junction with the Newry, Warrenpoint & Rostrevor Railway just beyond its Kilmorey Street terminus. The line opened on the 2 September 1861. A new station was built for the NW&RR at Dublin Bridge, which the company used from opening, closing their Kilmorey Street station on the same day. The old station carried on as a goods depot until about 1900. However, disagreements over working arrangements meant that through working didn't start until later in the year.

A TI class 4-4-2T, No. 185, built by Beyer Peacock in 1913, shunts around its train at Warrenpoint Station, 18 April 1953. Warrenpoint was a popular seaside destination, as the provision of the carriage sidings shows. The short spur to the quay can be seen curving through the gateposts on the right.

The Newry & Enniskillen Railway changed its name and aspirations with its extension from Goraghwood to Armagh, becoming the Newry & Armagh Railway. It merged with the GNR(I) on 30 June 1879, but it took until 4 June 1886 until the NW&RR also amalgamated with the GNR(I) and the whole route was under the control of one company with through trains running to Portadown and Belfast. In 1891, a new station at Warrenpoint was opened by the GNR(I), some seven chains nearer to Newry. The line was quite busy serving the port of Newry, especially with coal traffic, and its later years are well remembered for the seaside excursion traffic to Warrenpoint. Eventually the line was closed by the UTA.

Warrenpoint – Rostrevor

Passenger service withdrawn	February 1915	*Stations closed*	*Date*
Distance	3.25 miles	Warrenpoint Railway Station	February 1915
Company	Warrenpoint & Rostrevor Tramways Company	Rostrevor	February 1915
		Mourne Hotel *	February 1915

The tram terminus at Rostrevor. The tramway ran from Warrenpoint to the Mourne Hotel which can be seen in the background. A further ¾ mile stretch of line went down to the quay.

* Renamed Great Northern Hotel in 1899.

Great Northern Railway (Ireland)

Rostrevor Hotel

Great Northern Hotel, Rostrevor Co Down.

Great Northern Hotel & Lough Shore Rostrevor.

An advertisement for the Great Northern Hotel at Rostrevor. Formally the Mourne Hotel, the establishment was renamed when the GNR(I) bought it in 1899.

The resort of Rostrevor had originally been intended to get a railway courtesy of the Newry, Warrenpoint & Rostrevor Railway company. However, the NW&RR never got around to constructing the 3 mile line to the town. The way was then left open for another concern to link Warrenpoint with Rostrevor, a feat accomplished by the Warrenpoint & Rostrevor Tramways Company. Opened on 1 August 1877, the 2 feet 10 inch gauge horse drawn tramway left the NW&RR station in Warrenpoint and followed the road to the Mourne Hotel in Rostrevor. A little later, in October of that year, a short goods extension was opened down to the quay. The tramway was quite successful and benefited from through bookings for both passengers and goods with the NW&RR. The GNR(I) bought the Mourne Hotel in 1899, whereupon the tramway terminus was also renamed. The hotel was sold in 1966. The demise of the line began with competition from the early motor charabancs and after a violent gale washed away a section of track in 1915 the tramway was closed.

Goraghwood – Armagh

Passenger service withdrawn	1 February 1933	*Stations closed*	*Date*
Distance	17.25 miles	Loughgilly	1897
Company	Great Northern Railway of Ireland	Glen Anne *	1 February 1933
		Markethill	1 February 1933
Stations closed	*Date*	Hamiltonsbawn	1 February 1933
Goraghwood	4 January 1965	Armagh	1 October 1957
Ballydougherty Halt	1 February 1933	* Known as Loughgilly until 1924.	

A GNR(I) V class 4-4-0 compound, No. 84 'Falcon', stands at the platform of Goraghwood Station with the 2.30 p.m. from Dublin, 18 April 1953. Built in 1932 by Beyer Peacock, these locomotives made a fine sight in their light blue livery. Fortunately, sister locomotive No. 85 'Merlin' is preserved in full working order.

On the 25 August 1864, the Newry & Armagh Railway opened its line from Goraghwood to a temporary station at Drummondmore, one mile short of the station at Armagh. Completion of the line to the town was made on the 13 February 1865, whereupon the temporary station closed. This single line ran parallel to the Dublin & Belfast Junction Railway main line at Goraghwood for a short distance before climbing and crossing over the main line, heading north-west over the hills to Armagh. The line then came to the longest tunnel in Ireland at Lissummon which was 1,759 yards long and then to Ballydougherty Halt, 3½ miles from the start, which opened in 1912. Further on was Loughgilly Tunnel (365 yards long) which partly fell in on 25 January 1914. No trains ran from Goraghwood to Markethill until repairs had been affected and the line reopened on the 1 May 1914. Loughgilly Station was the next stop. Opened with the line, this station closed in 1897, being replaced by another station by the same name half a mile away (this was renamed Glen Anne Station in 1924). The quaint horse-drawn Glen Anne & Loughgilly Tramway met the Newry & Armagh Railway here and terminated between the running line and a siding. The tramway, built to a gauge of 1 foot 10 inches and opened in 1897, ran from the Glen Anne Works of George Gray & Sons and was used to transport coal to the works and linen from them. It closed in 1917.

Markethill Station.

The next station along the line was at Markethill, 8½ miles from Goraghwood. Four miles further on was Hamiltonsbawn Station and just 2¼ miles from Hamiltonsbawn is Derry's Crossing. It was here on 12 June 1889 that an overloaded fifteen-coach train bound for Warrenpoint stalled on the 1:75 incline some 700 yards short of the summit. In an effort to get the train moving again the rear ten coaches were uncoupled, the idea being that the locomotive would take the five coaches to the top and come back for the remaining ones. However, when the train tried to restart it moved backwards momentarily, pushing the ten uncoupled coaches. The brakes on these carriages were insufficient to hold them and they started to run downhill, gradually picking up speed. The system of train operation in use at the time was the 'time interval method'. A train was allowed a certain amount of time to traverse a section and another train would not be forwarded until that time had elapsed. As fate would have it, another train was waiting at Markethill for this interval to pass before being despatched. The station staff at Markethill were unaware of the problems being encountered by the previous train and duly sent off the next one at the appropriate time. This second train started to climb the incline and collided with the runaway carriages, killing 88 people. The disaster had a profound effect on railway operation and led to the passing of the Regulation of Railways Act in August of that year.

From Markethill, the line continued to Armagh where the Newry & Armagh Railway terminated at the Ulster Railway station. With the amalgamations of 1876, the company found itself having to use the GNR(I) stations at both Goraghwood and Armagh. Three more difficult years were to pass until the Newry & Armagh Railway became part of the GNR(I) on 30 June 1879. The GNR(I) continued to operate the line until the strike of 1933, which put an end to the passenger service and goods services from Markethill to Armagh. The remainder of the line finally closed 22 years later.

Armagh – Castleblayney

Passenger service withdrawn	1 January 1932 (Armagh to Keady)		
	2 April 1923 (Keady to Castleblayney)		
Distance	18.75 miles		
Company	Great Northern Railway of Ireland		

Stations closed	Date	Stations closed	Date
Armagh	1 October 1957	Milford	1 January 1932
Irish Street Halt	1 January 1932	Ballyards Halt	1 January 1932
		Tassagh Halt	1 January 1932
		Keady	1 January 1932
		Carnagh	2 April 1923
		Creaghanroe *	2 April 1923
		Castleblayney *	2 April 1923

The first rail excursion from Keady, photographed around 1907 when the line was still being built. 'Mullinger' was the contractor's locomotive. Built by Hunslet, this 0-6-0T was taken into GNR(I) stock as No. 204 in 1913 and renumbered in 1915. It was withdrawn in 1930. Note the makeshift buffers, not to mention the carriages!

* These two stations were on the six miles of the line that went into Co. Monaghan. Castleblayney remained open to services on the Dundalk–Londonderry route until 14 October 1957.

The first passenger train from Armagh arrives at Keady on 31 May 1909. It was hauled by a GNR(I) BT class 4-4-0T.

This line has one of the shortest operating histories in Ireland at just under thirteen years for its southern section. Built by the Castleblayney, Keady & Armagh Railway, the first section from Armagh to Keady was opened to goods traffic in 1908 and to passenger traffic on 31 May 1909. The remaining section to Castleblayney opened on 10 November 1910. A year later the line was absorbed into the GNR(I). The route south from Armagh took the line over some rugged and hilly countryside, necessitating three major viaducts – Ballyards just north of Ballyards Halt, Tassagh Viaduct north of Tassagh Halt and Keady Viaduct, south of Keady Station. The most impressive of these was Tassagh Viaduct, with its eleven arches spanning 570 feet. The massive concrete piers topped with brick faced arches still stand today.

Starting in Armagh, some 136 feet above sea level, the line steadily climbed its way at 1:70 for much of the way to Keady and from there climbed further still to reach 613 feet, the highest point on the GNR(I) system, south of Carnagh. From here, the line gradually descended to Castleblayney. The line served numerous small towns involved in the linen industry, many mills having their own private sidings. At the southern end, the line crossed into Co. Monaghan where it terminated in a bay platform at Castleblayney, on the Dundalk to Londonderry line. Connection to the main line was via a siding. Never a success, the southern section of the line from Keady to Castleblayney succumbed on 2 April 1923 when the GNR(I) discontinued its services completely. One of the problems with this part of the line was that from 1921 it crossed the border into the Irish Free State. This meant traffic on the line was now subject to customs inspections and the expense and delays caused by these were hardly worthwhile for the amount of traffic. The remaining half of the line struggled on for another nine years before it lost its passenger service on 1 January 1932. The Armagh to Keady section remained open to goods services until 1 October 1957 when the financially troubled Great Northern Railway Board called it a day and closed the line completely.

Keady Viaduct, south of the station, was opened for use on 10 November 1910. This 6 arch concrete viaduct had a very short life as the line south of Keady closed just 13 years later.

Portadown – Tynan

Stations closed	Date
Passenger service withdrawn	1 October 1957
Distance	17.75 miles
Company	Great Northern Railway of Ireland

Stations closed	Date
Richhill	1 October 1957
Retreat Halt	1 October 1957

Stations closed	Date
Armagh *	1 October 1957
Killylea	1 October 1957
Tynan **	1 October 1957

* Known as Armagh Railway Street in the 1910s and '20s
** Known as Tynan, Caledon & Middletown until 1880 and then as Tynan & Caledon.

Having built the line from Belfast to Portadown, the Ulster Railway continued to extend their line to Armagh. This meant crossing the River Bann and the opportunity was taken to build a larger station to the south of the river. The new line and station was opened for traffic on 1 March 1848 along with one intermediate station at Richhill. Another few years passed before the directors of the Ulster Railway decided to extend the line again, this time to Monaghan. The line was opened on 25 May 1858 with stations at Tynan and Glaslough. Killylea was opened a year later in 1859. The Ulster Railway amalgamated with the Northern Railway on 1 January 1876 to form the GNR(I). The station at Tynan on the Monaghan extension became the starting point for the Clogher Valley Railway on 2 May 1887. The Clogher Valley Railway was a 3 feet gauge line that wound its way through Counties Tyrone and Fermanagh, meeting back up with the GNR(I) at Maguiresbridge. The route was extended over the years to Clones where it joined the Irish North Western Railway on its way from Dundalk to Londonderry. Partition disrupted the natural traffic flows along this route and the line was singled to Richhill in 1934, the remaining double track section to Portadown being used to service the Metal Box Co. factory at Brownstown Crossing. In 1936, the level crossing at Quakers Crossing between Richhill and Armagh became a formal stop and was renamed Retreat Halt. Lasting up to closure, Retreat Halt was never given a platform. The final demise of the line came when the Great Northern Railway Board discontinued traffic along the route on 1 October 1957. The Brownstown section was retained and worked as a siding by the UTA until 4 January 1965.

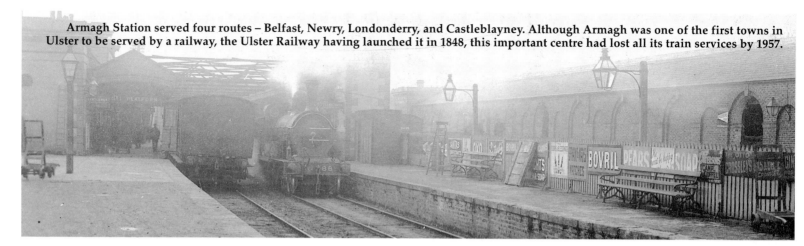

Armagh Station served four routes – Belfast, Newry, Londonderry, and Castleblayney. Although Armagh was one of the first towns in Ulster to be served by a railway, the Ulster Railway having launched it in 1848, this important centre had lost all its train services by 1957.

Portadown – Vernersbridge

Passenger service withdrawn	15 February 1965	Stations closed	Date
Distance	9.25 miles	Annaghmore	15 February 1965
Company	Great Northern Railway of Ireland	Derrycoose Crossing *	1 January 1957
		Vernersbridge **	20 September 1954
Stations closed	Date	* Railcar stop from 1936/37 to 1 January 1957.	
Annakeera Crossing *	1 January 1957	** Formerly known as Verner and renamed in December 1858.	

This route was part of a much larger scheme to connect Belfast with Londonderry. The first section of the 'Derry Road', as the line became known, was built by the Portadown, Dungannon & Omagh Railway, a concern financially backed by the Ulster Railway. Opened on 5 April 1858, the line left Portadown and swung west across the low lying boggy ground south of Lough Neagh. The first stop was Annaghmore, an area renowned for its large peat workings and still partially in use today. Some nine miles from there it arrived at Vernersbridge. Here the line crossed the River Blackwater on Blackwater Viaduct into Co. Tyrone. Approval for the use of the junction at Portadown was delayed until 4 July so in the meantime a temporary platform just west of the junction was used. The line to Londonderry was open throughout on 2 September 1861, whereupon it was leased to the Ulster Railway for 999 years. However, the Portadown, Dungannon & Omagh Railway and the Ulster Railway amalgamated on 1 January 1876 with the Northern Railway to form the GNR(I). The route enabled the newly formed company to offer an alternative through route from Belfast to Londonderry to that of the Belfast & Northern Counties Railway via Coleraine. In the 1930s, the GNR(I) investigated various economies to help compete with burgeoning road competition and one of these was the use of railcars and railbuses. Railcars were used on the Derry Road and enabled the company to pick up and set down passengers at, amongst other places, various designated road level crossings. Annakeera and Derrycoose Crossings became designated stops. Suffering post-war financial difficulties, the GNR(I) was reformed into the Great Northern Railway Board on 1 September 1953. This didn't help the station at Vernersbridge, which closed on 20 September 1954. The difficulties still continued and the GNRB was divided between CIE and the UTA on 1 October 1958. The GNRB's railcar stops at various level crossings had already ceased on 1 January 1957. The line continued to be substantially busy under the UTA, but they eventually decided to close the line on 4 January 1965. However, this was deferred and the Derry Road closed completely on 15 February 1965.

Closed passenger stations on lines still open to passengers

Line/Service	**Dublin – Belfast**

Stations closed	Date
Adavoyle	1933
Wellington Inn	1852
Newry *	1942
Newry Armagh Road **	c.1856
Goraghwood	4 January 1965

Stations closed	Date
Knockarny Crossing ***	4 January 1965
Augheranter Crossing ***	June 1955
Acton Crossing ***	Date unknown
Tanderagee ****	4 January 1965
Portadown (first)	1848
Portadown (second) *****	1863
Portadown (third)	5 October 1970

Tanderagee Station.

* Newry Station opened in 1855. It was later called Monaghan Road, then Newry Main Line, then Bessbrook. It was reopened as Newry in May 1984.
** Named Mullaghglass until 1854.
*** Railcar stops.

**** Originally named Madden Bridge, then Tanderagee and Gilford. Known as Tanderagee from 1894.
***** The current Portadown Station is the fourth, built almost on the site as the second.

Line/Service		**Dublin – Belfast** (continued)		Stations closed	Date

Line/Service		**Dublin – Belfast** (continued)

Stations closed	Date
Seagoe	1842
Goodyear	30 October 1983
Pritchard's Bridge	1844
Damhead *	2 July 1973

Stations closed	Date
The Damhead	1844
Broomhenge	1953
Maze **	1 July 1974
Knockmore Junction Halt ***	1946
Ulster Junction ****	30 November 1885
Belfast Great Victoria Street *****	26 April 1976

A Sharp Stewart B class 0-6-0, No. 62 'Tyrone', passing through Tanderagee Station with a mixed freight.

* Opened on the same site as The Damhead in 1935.
** Originally named Maze Platform.
*** This had originally been closed in 1933/34, but reopened in 1945.

**** An exchange platform which was also called Belfast Central Junction.
***** The current station of this name was built a little further west of the original site and opened on 20 September 1995.

Qs class 4-4-0 No. 124 'Cerebus', built by Neilson Reid in 1902, stands in the third Portadown Station, *c.*1914. This station closed in 1970 and was replaced by a new, more basic facility south of the River Bann.

An SG2 0-6-0, No. 40, shunting at Portadown Station, 3 June 1961. This was built by Nasmyth Wilson as GNR(I) No. 10 in 1924. An ex-GNR(I) railcar set stands in the adjacent platform.